The Little Book of Big Bold Prayers

100 Days of Leveling Up Your Prayer Life

Jennifer
Keep the Faith
Prayer changes
everything.
Pink and green
Hugs & Kisses
Love ya
LS
Fatima

ISBN:1533469555
ISBN-13: 9781533469557

DEDICATION

January 2013 should have been the beginning of the best year of my life. I just released my second book, "Boss Lady: Seven Life Principles to Reign in the New Economy." I was back to work after taking some time off and I was living in a new space that would allow my disabled mother with multiple sclerosis to get around with no problem.

Everything looked as if it was finally coming together. Then, that dreadful day came, changing my life forever! On January 10, 2013, I was teaching a class of social workers when I got the call. The call was like the shot heard around the world. My brother said the words I never wanted to hear. He said, "You have to come home. Please come home. Mommy is gone." I heard the words, but they were unreal. I let out a scream that will always be embedded in the minds of those who heard me, embedded in the minds of my students who instantly came to my rescue. I remember falling on the floor screaming, "I don't believe it."

What I remember most about that day was my students kneeling on the floor and praying for me in different languages, rubbing my head and consoling me. I had to be carried out of work that dreadful day. And my new normal without my Queen mother began.

My mother was a prayer warrior. She prayed about everything and worried about nothing. Her faith has strengthened my faith and taught me that trusting in God through my good times and not so good times is the way to true happiness.

In Loving Memory of

Sylvia Denise McCarter

I Love You Mommy

CONTENTS

ACKNOWLEDGMENTS

PRAYER WARRIORS

when two or more come together in his name

Thank you to my Prayer Warriors who are constantly praying with and for me. May the favor of God rest richly upon you.

For my husband Les, My son Jordan,

My earthly father Robert Sr. and brother Robert Jr.,

My sisters Sylvia Jr., Nicky, Misha, Heather, Carla,

Halima, Karen, Debra, Dena and Dottie

FORWARD

Prayer is like a message you send to God. Then, He will try to respond to that message as soon as possible. The first time I remember praying was when my two grandmother's passed. I was praying and hoping they would look down on me from above. I was praying for them to be okay and giving my mom and dad their strength when they needed it. In the winter time, when I didn't want school to be open, I would pray for snow so I could play my game. Those were the fun prayers. Every time before a football game, I would pray to God to protect my body so that I would not get hurt. Prayer is important because it keeps us in contact with Him. We should pray to God, saying, "Thank you, Lord, for waking us up or at night saying thank you, God, for a good day.

Jordan Scipio, 12 years old

Dear Reader,

Now is the time to be Bold! I want to show you how to use God's word to decree and declare every promise that He has for your life. I want to teach you how to pray for people and circumstances that seek to harm you by using powerful words that will send the enemy shaking.

Are you ready to level up your prayer life? Are you ready to walk in the authority granted to you by God? Are you ready to speak boldly over your life, family and friends? I pray this book will bless you beyond your wildest dreams and for God to get all the Glory.

Are you Ready? I hope you are.

Many Blessings,

Fatima Scipio

BIG BOLD FAITH

"I tell you the truth, if you had faith even as small as a mustard seed, you could say to this mountain, 'Move from here to there', and it would move. Nothing would be impossible."

This Big Bold Book of Prayers is all about using your faith to get your mouth in alignment with the promises of God. The time is now for us to train and force our mouths into speaking things that be not as though they were. No longer will we, as children of God, allow setbacks, trials, and tribulations to dictate our future. This book will get your mouthpiece and mind on a pathway to leveling up your prayer life and living the life God has purposed us to live.

My own journey to developing my faith muscles started over twenty years ago. I thought I had it all together until the day my mother passed away. The days, weeks, months after her passing left me in a state of depression. The loss left a big hole in my life and left me wondering how I would go on without my best friend. I knew she was not coming back. I knew I would never physically speak to her again, and I just couldn't understand it.

Giving up on life was not an option. I had a family. Turning to other coping mechanisms was not an option because they could lead to death. So, I went inside. I went inside myself and withdrew mentally. Then, one night while I was crying, my son who was around seven or eight years old came and wiped the tears from my eyes with his little hands, telling me it was going to be okay. This touch, so endearing and innocent, breathed life into me once again. I hugged him tightly and thanked him. Immediately,

I grabbed my journal and wrote "God Help Me."

My faith was shattered. I started writing all my feelings down, having conversations with God, allowing myself to be naked before him. I was vulnerable in every way possible. And in my alone time, flashbacks of my mother's voice played over and over like a tape recorder in my head. I heard her say, "God's got you. Eh, Don't Worry. My God is good." Remembering her words gave me comfort and praying brought me closer to God.

Fast forward to today. I see how God has opened many doors and closed many doors. Prayer has helped me to accept things I will never understand and helped me to go boldly before God using His word. All He wants is for us to have a deeper relationship with Him, which happens through the act of prayer. Praying happens by knowing His word. Knowing His word produces Faith.

Day 1

Scripture

"The word is truth and when we follow it we are made free."

- John 8:32

Prayer

Dear God,

I thank You for Your word. I thank You that Your word is truth, and because it is truth, when we follow it we are made free.

Thank You for this promise.

Reflection: Use space below to jot down your thoughts.

Day 2

Scripture

"Your word is a lamp for my feet, a light on my path.

-Psalm 119:105

Prayer

Dear God,

Thank you for guiding me in the way I should go. Because Your word is a lamp for my feet, I have clear vision of where I am headed.

Reflection: Use space below to jot down your thoughts.

Day 3

Scripture

"The word protects us."

- Psalm 18:30

Prayer

Dear God,

I thank You for the protection that comes from Your word. Thank You for the word that protects my family and me. I know and believe that Your way is perfect. Your word has been proven time and time again. Your word never fails. I thank You that it is a shield to all who trust in You. I trust in You, Lord, and You alone.

Reflection: Use space below to jot down your thoughts.

Day 4

Scripture

"Meditating on the word brings wisdom, prosperity, and success."

- Joshua 1:8

Prayer

Dear God,

Thank You your word.

Thank You for wisdom.

Thank You for prosperity.

Thank You for good success.

Reflection: Use space below to jot down your thoughts.

Day 5

Scripture

"Those who order their conduct and conversations according to the word are blessed."

- Psalm 119:2

Prayer

Dear God,

Let my behavior and conversations get in alignment with Your word. Let all that I say and do be blessed.

Reflection: Use space below to jot down your thoughts.

Day 6

Scripture

"God's word gives us good judgement, wise and right discernment, and knowledge."

- Psalm 119:66

Prayer

Dear God,

Thank You for Your powerful word that gives me good judgement. Your powerful word that makes me wise and gives me good discernment and knowledge.

Reflection: Use space below to jot down your thoughts.

Day 7

Scripture

"Trust in the Lord and do good; dwell in the land and enjoy safe pasture. Take delight in the Lord and He will give you the desires of your heart."

- Psalm 37:3-4

Prayer

Dear God,

I put my trust in You. My only desire is to do good, live safely, and prosper. Help me to feed on your faithfulness. Let me take delight in You, Lord. Thank You for giving me the desires of my heart. I commit everything I do to You, Lord. I trust You and I am grateful for Your help. Help me to rest in You, Lord that I may wait patiently for You. Help me to cease from anger understanding that it only causes harm. I know that those who wait on You will inherit the earth and shall delight in the abundance of peace. I thank You that my steps are ordered by You. I thank You for being my strength in the time of trouble.

Reflection: Use space below to jot down your thoughts.

Day 8

Scripture

"But let him ask in faith, nothing wavering. For he that wavereth is like a wave of the sea driven with the wind and tossed."

- James 1:6

Prayer

Dear God,

I come humbly before You thanking You that I owe nothing to anyone except to love them. I know that if I love my neighbor, I will fulfill the requirement of Your law. Lord I thank You for generously providing all I need. I thank You that I will always have everything I need and plenty left over to share with others. Lord, give me wisdom. For You are generous and I thank You in advance. Lord, help me to truly have faith in You alone. Let me not waver, for it is written that a person with a divided loyalty is unsettled as a wave of the sea that is blown and tossed by the wind. I do not want to be among those who should not expect anything from You. I do not want my loyalty to be divided between You and the things of this world. I do not want to be unstable in everything I do, but have a firm foundation in You, O God.

Reflection: Use space below to jot down your thoughts.

Day 9

Scripture

"Have I not commanded you? Be strong and courageous. Do not be afraid: do not be discouraged, for the Lord your God will be with you wherever you go."

- Joshua 1:9

Prayer

Lord,

Use me. Tell me. Show me what You want me to do. I know victory comes through faith in God and obedience to Your word rather than military might or numerical superiority. I will be strong and of good courage. I will meditate on Your word day and night. My desire is to know You and have a relationship with You. I want to bring glory to Your name by how I live my life. This life is not about me; It's all about You, God.

Reflection: Use space below to jot down your thoughts.

Day 10

Scripture

"And he said to them, 'Take care and be on your guard against all covetousness, for one's life does not consist in the abundance of his possessions.' Then he said 'Beware, guard against every kind of greed. Life is not measured by how much you own.'"

- Luke 12:15

Prayer

Lord, I can do nothing of myself

I just rest in You, Lord.

I trust You.

I commit my salary over to You.

I commit my anxiety over to You.

I commit my finances over to You.

I commit

___

I commit

____

I commit

____

God, You are in control.

Thank You, God

Reflection: Use space below to jot down your thoughts.

Day 11

Scripture

"Peace I leave with you; my peace I give you. I do not give to you as the world gives. Do not let your hearts be troubled and do not be afraid."

- John 14:27

Prayer

Dear God,

I give You my fear of not having enough in exchange for Your peace.

I give You my fear of not living out my potential in exchange for Your peace.

I give You my fear of my family being harmed in exchange for Your peace.

I give You my fear of missing opportunities in exchange for Your peace.

I lay all that I am on the table, Lord. I cannot win without You.

Reflection: Use space below to jot down your thoughts.

Day 12

Scripture

"You will seek Me and find Me when you seek Me with all your heart."

- Jeremiah 29:13

Prayer

Lord,

Keep me focused on You.

Let me not be moved by distractions.

Let me remember Your promises.

My Faith is in You, not man.

Let me protect my brain space with Your word.

Anything that is not of You must go.

I am open to Your guidance and will for my life.

I am Your workmanship, created in Christ Jesus to do good works.

I am Your masterpiece.

Reflection: Use space below to jot down your thoughts.

Day 13

Scripture

"This is the confidence we have in approaching God: that is we ask anything according to His will, He hears us."

- 1 John 5:14

Prayer

Dear God,

Thank You for hearing me.

Help me to consistently examine my life and heart so that my prayers are not hindered but aligned with Your will.

I trust You, Lord.

As I seek Your will for my decisions, I will

1. Pray without ceasing.
2. Pray with persistent pleas.
3. Test my decisions against scripture
4. Fast
5. Seek Godly counsel

6. Remain Faithful and open to correction
7. Be a mouthpiece for you

Reflection: Use space below to jot down your thoughts.

Day 14

Scripture

"Knowing this, that the trying of your faith worketh patience. But let patience have her perfect work, that ye may be perfect and entire, wanting nothing."

- James 1:3-4

Prayer

Dear God,

Let me count it all joy when I fall into my trials,

Knowing that the testing of my faith produces patience.

Lord, let my patience have its perfect work that I may be perfect and complete, lacking nothing.

Reflection: Use space below to jot down your thoughts.

Day 15

Scripture

"But from there you will seek the Lord your God and you will find Him, if you search after Him with all of your heart and with all your soul."

- Deuteronomy 4:29

Prayer

Abba Father,

Early I seek Thee.

Show me a glimpse of what's to come.

Show me in my dreams.

Thank You, God.

Reflection: Use space below to jot down your thoughts.

THANK YOU LORD

PURPOSELY ON PURPOSE

"After the death of Moses, the Lord's servant, the Lord spoke to Joshua and said, 'Moses my servant is dead. Therefore, the time has come for you to lead these people into the land I am giving them.'"

Joshua 1:1-2

You come across a quote that reads "Twenty years from now you will be more disappointed by the things you didn't do than by the ones you did do."- Mark Twain.

For some time now, you have been having an ongoing battle in your mind about whether or not you should leave your nine to five job where you have worked for twelve years. If you stay, you can retire from a stable job, and most likely not fully use all of your talents and gifts that God has given you. If you leave, twenty years from now you will most likely have done much more because you took the leap of Faith to pursue your dreams.

For some people, the answer seems obviously clear, and yet many people find themselves quite understandably in a very scary place. You have to make a decision, and not only does your decision impact you but also all areas of your life.

There are countless stories in the bible about decisions people had to make solely based on faith. Moses had to decide to confront pharaoh about his treatment of the Israelites. Noah had to decide to build the Ark despite what people may have thought. And, Abraham had to decide to leave everything he had and go into the unknown. The key words in what these men had to do are Confront, Build, and Leave. Being purposely on purpose will require you to confront your fears, build your relationship with God, and develop the vision he has given you about your life. Lastly, you may have to leave your comfort zone and some familiar things behind.

When you follow God's will, then you will receive the promise. We often tend to plead with God to give the promise when we haven't done the work. Getting to your Promise requires you to live purposefully. Living purposely means everything you do is in accordance to serving God's plan for your life. Now is the time for you to start intentionally living. The time has come for you to lead. Maybe God needs you to serve as the principal of a school or, better yet, build your own school. What are you intentionally doing to ensure that you do those things? For me, I had to make sure that when I took the leap, everything I did was intentional towards my desire to "create."

Day 16

Scripture

"Every place that the sole of your foot shall tread upon, that have I given unto you, as I said unto Moses."

- Joshua 1:3

Prayer

Dear God,

I thank You that every place the sole of my feet shall walk You have given me.

I thank You that from the city to the country what is for me is for me.

I thank You for helping me to be strong and courageous as the obstacles attempt to guide me off course.

I thank You for trusting me to lead and help others.

Help me to be careful and obey all of your instructions.

Reflection: Use space below to jot down your thoughts.

Day 17

Scripture

"Study this book of instruction continually. Meditate on it day and night so you will be sure to obey everything in it. Only then will you prosper and succeed in all you do."

- Joshua 1:7-8

Prayer

Dear God,

Help me to focus and meditate on Your word day and night. I understand that Your word will lead me to prosper and have good success.

Thank You

Reflection: Use space below to jot down your thoughts.

Day 18

Scripture

"But you are a chosen people, a royal priesthood, a holy nation, God's special possession, that you may declare the praises of Him who called you out of darkness into His wonderful light."

- 1 Peter 2:9

Prayer

Father,

I thank You that I am Your chosen.

I thank You that I am royalty apart of Your holy nation.

I thank You that I am Your special possession.

I thank You for calling me out of darkness and into this wonderful light.

Reflection: Use space below to jot down your thoughts.

Day 19

Scripture

"There is a time for everything, and a season for every activity under the heavens."

- Ecclesiastes 3:1

Prayer

Dear God,

I understand there is a time for everything.

A time to be happy

A time to be sad

A time for work

A time for play

A time to stay

A time to go

Lord, I thank You for being my rock through all the seasons of my life.

Reflection: Use space below to jot down your thoughts.

Day 20

Scripture

"'For I know the plans I have for you,' declares the Lord, 'plans to prosper you and not to harm you, plans to give you hope and future.'"

- Jeremiah 29:11

Prayer

Dear God,

Thank You for making plans for me.

Thank You for the plan for me to prosper

Thank you for giving me hope

And a future.

Reflection: Use space below to jot down your thoughts.

Day 21

Scripture

"Many are the plans in a person's heart, but it is the Lord's purpose that prevails."

- Proverbs 19:21

Prayer

Dear God,

I know I may have my own plans in my heart, but I know that above everything I can think of, Your purpose for me is greater.

Reflection: Use space below to jot down your thoughts.

Day 22

Scripture

"And we know that in all things, God works for the good of those who love Him, who have been called according to his purpose."

- Romans 8:28

Prayer

Lord,

Thank You for working for my good.

For I am Your handiwork created to do good.

Thank You for preparing me for such a time as this.

Reflection: Use space below to jot down your thoughts.

Day 23

Scripture

"Pride leads to disgrace but with humility comes wisdom."

- Proverbs 11:2

Prayer

Dear God,

Let wisdom guide me in all of my decisions.

Reflection: Use space below to jot down your thoughts.

Day 24

Scripture

"Take delight in the Lord and He will give you your hearts desires."

- Psalm 37:4

Prayer

Dear God,

Lord, let me truly find peace and fulfillment in You.

Lord, let me place my joy and hope in You, first.

Reflection: Use space below to jot down your thoughts.

Day 25

Scripture

"Be still before the Lord and wait patiently for Him; do not fret when people succeed in their ways."

- Psalm 37:7

Prayer

Dear God,

I commit my ways to you. Thank You for making my reward shine like the sun.

Let me be patient and wait on You.

Let me not worry about others' success, but keep my eyes on you.

Reflection: Use space below to jot down your thoughts.

Day 26

Scripture

"The Lord makes firm the steps of the one who delights in Him; though He may stumble, He will not fall, for the Lord upholds Him with His hand.

- Psalm 37:23-24

Prayer

Father,

Thank You for making my steps firm.

Though I may stumble

Though obstacles may come

I know You uphold me with Your heavenly hand.

Reflection: Use space below to jot down your thoughts.

Day 27

Scripture

"I know that You can do all things and that no plan of Yours can be thwarted."

- Job 42:2

Prayer

Lord,

I know that You can do everything and no one and nothing can stop You.

Let me remember this when I feel like the walls are closing in on me.

Let me remember this when the strain of life tries to grab me by the neck.

Let me remember this when I feel like I am mentally drowning.

For Your word is truth.

Reflection: Use space below to jot down your thoughts.

Day 28

Scripture

"All scripture is God breathed and is useful for teaching, rebuking, correcting and training in righteousness, so that the servant of God may be thoroughly equipped for every good work."

- 2 Timothy 3:16

Prayer

Dear God,

Thank You for Your inspiring word. Through it I am complete and equipped for every good work.

Reflection: Use space below to jot down your thoughts.

Day 29

Scripture

"Joyful are those you discipline, Lord, those You teach with Your instructions."

- Psalm 94:12

Prayer

Dear God,

Help me to change. Help me to be more disciplined and have self-control. Help me to have enough faith in You to bring about the changes I want to see in my life. Help me to make the right choices and develop new habits that will bring me the life You have destined me to live. Let me lean on You to change my life, for I know apart from You I can do nothing. Lord I cannot do anything if You don't make it happen. Let me be responsible for my actions. Let me discipline myself according to Your word. Let me be wise and think about the consequences of my actions. Let me care more about later than about reacting right now. Let me look at discipline and self-control as major components to having good health, prosperity, peace, good relationships, and fulfilling my purpose in this life.

Reflection: Use space below to jot down your thoughts.

Day 30

Scripture

"The word brings stability, fruitfulness, and fulfillment and all that I do will prosper."

- Psalm 1:3

Prayer

Dear God,

Thank You for Your word that brings stability. Let the things that are unstable in my life fall in line with Your word.

Thank You for fruitfulness. Let me bear fruit in all areas of my life according to Your word.

Thank You for fulfillment. Let me be full from Your word.

And thank You for making all that I do prosper.

Reflection: Use space below to jot down your thoughts.

Day 31

Scripture

"God's word has the power to create."

- Genesis 1

Prayer

Dear God,

Your word is so powerful. You spoke life and formed the heavens and the earth and everything in it. Because I was made in your image, I, too, can speak life and create the things I want to see manifest.

Reflection: Use space below to jot down your thoughts.

Day 32

Scripture

"God's word enables us to walk at liberty and at ease."

- Psalm 119:45

Prayer

Dear God,

I am so grateful that Your word allows me to walk freely and at ease. I am not bound by anyone or anything.

Reflection: Use space below to jot down your thoughts.

Day 33

Scripture

"For the Lord grants wisdom! From His mouth come knowledge and understanding."

- Proverbs 2:6

Prayer

Dear God,

Thank You for wisdom. Thank You for making me wiser than all who come up against me. I thank You that I am two steps ahead, winning in all areas of my life. I thank You that all I have in my hand will prosper because of the wisdom You have given me.

Reflection: Use space below to jot down your thoughts.

Day 34

Scripture

"Do not merely listen to the word, and so deceive yourselves. Do what it says."

- James 1: 22

Prayer

Dear God,

Let me be a doer of the word, not just a hearer. That by being a doer, the word will take root in me and save my soul.

Reflection: Use space below to jot down your thoughts.

Day 35

Scripture

"Be strong and courageous. Do not be afraid or terrified because of them, for the Lord your God goes with you; He will never leave you nor forsake you.

- Deuteronomy 31:6

Prayer

Dear God,

I am so grateful for Your word and the protection it provides me against evil.

I thank You for the boldness that the word gives me to speak and walk in the authority that comes from You.

Reflection: Use space below to jot down your thoughts.

Day 36

Scripture

"Do not be conformed to this present world, but be transformed by the renewing of your mind, so that you may test and approve what is the will of God."

- Romans 12:2

Prayer

Heavenly Father,

I genuinely acknowledge that I only know and understand partially while You know and understand everything perfectly. I pray that You give me what it takes, so I can strive to make sure that I am at the center of Your will. Whatever vision and goals I have are guaranteed to come to pass if they are consistent with Your perfect will. I pray to be totally reliant on You, knowing that You are fully able to do for me and my family what is in Your perfect will and timing for Your own glory.

Reflection: Use space below to jot down your thoughts.

Day 37

Scripture

"Whether you turn to the right or to the left, your ears will hear a voice behind you saying, 'This is the way, walk in it.'"

- Isaiah 30:21

Prayer

Lord,

The desire to do more is nothing if You are not in it.

May You guide my steps.

May my ears hear.

May my fears diminish

May my finances be more than enough.

May I walk in love and wisdom

God what must I do today?

Guide me.

Reflection: Use space below to jot down your thoughts.

Day 38

Scripture

"And his master saw that the Lord was with him and that the Lord made all he did prosper in his hand. So Joseph found favor in his sight." – Genesis 39:3-4

"For You, O Lord, will bless the righteous with favor, You will surround him as with a shield." – Psalm 5:12

"You prepare a table before me in the presence of my enemies; You anoint my head with oil; my cup runs over, surely goodness and mercy shall follow me all the days of my life; and I will dwell in the house of the Lord forever." –Psalms 23:5-6

Prayer

Lord,

Go before me. Let those who have ears hear how great and amazing I am. May my cup run over and bless lives. Lord, give me favor.

Lord, I pray that people see You in me. I thank You in advance for making all that I do prosper.

I thank You for Your divine favor.

Reflection: Use space below to jot down your thoughts.

Day 39

Scripture

"Hope deferred makes the heart sick, but a dream fulfilled is a tree of life."

- Proverbs 13:12

So many of us get very disappointed when it looks like what we most desire will not come to fruition. From our standing point, what we have been dreaming about looks as if it was just a dream. This scripture says Hope deferred, not hope destroyed. It just means that maybe now is not the appointed time. What we must do is not allow the deferment to leave us depleted and broken down. We must continue to press toward the mark in Jesus Christ.

Prayer

Dear God,

I thank You that my hopes and dreams will come in just the right time that You have set. I thank You for the courage to wait patiently on You.

Reflection: Use space below to jot down your thoughts.

Day 40

Scripture

"Commit your actions to the Lord and your plans will succeed."

- Proverbs 16:3

Prayer

Lord,

I surrender to You. My plans are (insert your plan). I wait patiently for Your reply. Lord, while pursuing my plans, I pray to hear Your voice. Bring my thoughts into agreement with Your will. Lord, let me live my life to win in Your name. I know that I run my own race and in competition with no one. I know You have put everyone on their own track, which means everyone can win his/her own race! I know in order for my plans to work, I must discipline my life, and I am ready.

Reflection: Use space below to jot down your thoughts.

Day 41

Scripture

"If you abide in Me and My words abide in you, you will ask what you desire and it shall be done for you."

- John 15:7

Prayer

Dear God,

I am blessed that You have fashioned me to bear fruit. I thank You for pruning me, getting rid of anything undesirable so that I can bare more fruit. In Your word You said, "If I abide in You, I can ask what I desire, and it shall be done for me." Thank You God.

Reflection: Use space below to jot down your thoughts.

Day 42

Scripture

"And I tell you, ask and it will be given to you; seek and you will find; Knock and it will be opened to you."

- Luke 11:9

Ask, Seek and Knock. Simple yet powerful words.

Ask requires us to muster up the courage to say what we really want.

Seek requires our eyes to see beyond what's on the surface. The answers and solutions we need are there, but we have to be committed to look without running out of patience.

Knock is an action. Are you really knocking on doors? Are you paying attention to the opportunities before you?

Ask, Seek, Knock. Embrace the power of these simple words.

Prayer

Dear God,

Hear my cry.

I am asking for

____

I am seeking

____

I am knocking on

____

Examples:

I am asking for opportunities to use my gifts and talents.

I am seeking wisdom that will guide me to make sound decisions

I am knocking on door of major opportunities and enlarging my territory

Reflection: Use space below to jot down your thoughts.

Day 43

Scripture

"The thief's purpose is to steal, kill, and destroy; My purpose is to give them a rich and satisfying life.

- John 10:10

Prayer

Lord,

Let me be able to discern the activities of the enemy that comes to steal, kill, and destroy my purpose.

Let me always guard my heart and renew my mind with your words to block, shut down, and speak life over myself and others.

Reflection: Use space below to jot down your thoughts.

THANK YOU LORD

GET READY FOR THE PROMISE LAND

"And I have promised to bring you up out of your oppression in Egypt. I will lead you to a land flowing with milk and honey"

- *Exodus 3:17*

When some think of the promise land, quite naturally we only think of it as a physical location. I want you to think of it first as a spiritual place in your mind. A place in your mind that is full of richness and abundance. A place flowing with purpose, ideas for good and being innovative. A beautiful place where you are committed to your relationship with God and ready to give up control and allow Him to sit on His throne in the driver's seat of your life.

What would you do if someone gave you an all-expense paid vacation? What if they told you to bring your suitcase with nothing in it because they were going to buy you everything you need? Would you do it?

Before continuing to read think about your answer, write Yes or No on this page and then continue reading on the next page.

My aunt Debra called me and asked if I wanted to go on vacation, everything planned and organized by her. When the time came, I packed my bags. Then, she told me to bring an empty suitcase because she would be taking me shopping. I had all kinds of thoughts running through my mind. So I decided to unpack and then wondered if she really meant not bring anything. So, I text her asking what about this and what about that. She said we would buy it. I scratched my head. I was confused and struggled with going to meet up with her with an empty suitcase. This was another level of faith and trust.

For a long time God has been showing me how I have had one foot in and one foot out when it comes to Faith. He tells us to cast our cares on to Him but for me the controlling person that I am found this extremely difficult. My internal battle and fight to release control over to an unknown situation was real. So, I unpacked everything except for some sandals and one bathing suit.

When I met up with her, she purchased everything

from head to toe. She had clothes, sandals, swimwear, you name it. Not only did she do this for me, but also for my son and nephew. She even went as far as flying one of my sisters to where we were vacationing after our cruise.

There were so many lessons in this interaction. First, it reminded me that God wants to show us His sovereignty. He wants to show off in our lives. He knows that some of us struggle with giving up control to the unknown, control over our trials and circumstances and yet He is reminding me that He watches over me. He uses people to show us his love and kindness. I bet my aunt didn't truly understand how God was using her to reveal this to me.

Secondly, God was showing that not only is He the great I AM to me, but his promise is to me, my children, and my children's children. So, the promises do not only benefit you, but also your family. With God, and in the words of Bruno Mars, you are dripping with finesse.

Lastly, your preparation gets you ready for the promised land, and preparation begins in your mind. Your mind has to be fertile ground for the promised land.

Day 44

Scripture

"The Lord's promises are pure, like silver refined in a furnace, purified seven times over."

- Psalm 12:6

Prayer

Dear God,

I am so thankful that Your word is filled with promises to give me mercy and grace. Let me keep Your word. Let me remember what it promises me even in the times of trials and tribulations. Let me walk in love knowing that Your mercy and grace endures forever.

Reflection: Use space below to jot down your thoughts.

Day 45

Scripture

"He gives strength to the weary and increases the power of the weak."

- Isaiah 40:29

Prayer

Dear God,

Thank You for giving me strength and increasing my power when I am weak.

Reflection: Use space below to jot down your thoughts.

Day 46

Scripture

"But those who hope in the Lord will renew their strength. They will soar on wings like eagles; they will run and not grow weary, they will walk and not be faint.

- Isaiah 40:31

Prayer

Lord,

My hope is in You. Thank You for renewing my strength.

Like an eagle, I will soar. Thank You for helping me take flight.

I will run and not grow weary. Thank You for the air that I breathe.

I will walk and not faint. Thank You for giving me strength.

Reflection: Use space below to jot down your thoughts.

Day 47

Scripture

"For God so loved the world that He gave His one and only son, that whoever believes in Him shall not perish but have eternal life.

- John 3:16

Prayer

Dear God,

Thank You for loving me so much that You gave Your only son that I may live.

Reflection: Use space below to jot down your thoughts.

Day 48

Scripture

"And my God will meet all your needs according to the riches of His glory in Christ Jesus."

- Philippians 4:19

Prayers

Dear God,

Thank You for meeting all my needs according to Your riches and glory in Christ Jesus. I decree and declare that all my needs are met.

Reflection: Use space below to jot down your thoughts.

Day 49

Scripture

"Even though I walk through the darkest valley, I will fear no evil, for You are with me; Your rod and Your staff, they comfort me."

- Psalm 23:4

Prayer

Dear God,

I know the trials may come, but Your word says You are with me.

I will fear no evil, because Your words says You are with me.

I am grateful for Your discipline and protection because Your word says Your rod and staff comfort me.

Reflection: Use space below to jot down your thoughts.

Day 50

Scripture

"The righteous cry out, and the Lord hears them; He delivers them from all their troubles."

- Psalm 34:17

Prayer

Lord,

When I cry out to You, thank You for hearing me.

Thank You for delivering me from all of my troubles.

Reflection: Use space below to jot down your thoughts.

Day 51

Scripture

"Sing to the Lord; praise the Lord. For He Has delivered the life of the needy from the hand of evildoers."

- Jeremiah 20:13

Prayer

Dear God,

I sing to You.

I praise You.

Thank You for delivering me from the hands of people and circumstances that seek to harm me.

Reflection: Use space below to jot down your thoughts.

Day 52

Scripture

"They are to do good, to be rich in good works, to be generous and ready to share, thus storing up treasure for the future, so that they may take hold of that which is truly life."

- 1 Timothy 6:18-19

Prayer

Lord,

Let me do good so that I am rich in good works.

Let me be generous and share, so that I may store up treasure in my future.

Let me remember what life is truly about.

Reflection: Use space below to jot down your thoughts.

Day 53

Scripture

“Therefore, if anyone is in Christ, he is a new creation. The old has passed away; behold, the new has come.”

- 2 Corinthians 5:17

Prayer

Dear God,

I am so grateful for Christ being in me.

I know because He is in me, I am new.

I know because He is in me, the old me has passed away.

Because He is in me, watch out world, the new me has come.

Reflection: Use space below to jot down your thoughts.

■■

Day 54

Scripture

"Do not be anxious about anything, but every situation, by prayer and petition with thanksgiving, present your requests to God."

- Philippians 4:6

Prayer

Dear God,

In your word You said I should be anxious for nothing.

In Your word You said I should come to You regarding every situation in my life.

In Your word You said I should come to You by prayer and petition, giving You thanks and submit my request to You, O God.

Lord, as I humbly come before You, I thank You for all of Your promises to me in advance.

Reflection: Use space below to jot down your thoughts.

THANK YOU LORD

POSSESING THE BLESSINGS

"Then the Lord said to Joshua, 'See I have delivered Jericho into your hands, along with its king and its fighting men. March around the city once with all the armed men. Do this for six days. Have seven priests carry trumpets of rams' horns in front of the ark. On the seventh day, march around the city seven times with the priests' blowing the trumpets. When you hear them sound a long blast on the trumpets, have the whole army give a loud shout; then the wall of the city will collapse and the army will go up, everyone straight in.'"

- *Joshua 6:2-5*

Going in for your blessings will not come without trials. Remember, there is always a battle going on in your mind. Your mind will focus on what you feed it. So, you have to make a conscious decision to really feed your mind the word of God so that you can withstand the challenges that come your way. But the good news is you are destined to win with God.

God is constantly working on your behalf. Even at times when it doesn't seem like it. He is an unconventional God. He doesn't always do things the way we expect them to be done.

I remember attending a church service and the pastor told a story about an atheist woman who didn't have any money or food. So, she said God, "If you really are God, and You are who people say You are, I'm praying for some food. I'm hungry, and I don't have any money." Well, little did the lady know, her next door neighbor who was also an atheist over heard her prayers to God. So, he chuckled, and left to go to the market. He returned to where they lived, placed the bag of groceries in front of her door, rang her door bell, and hid. The lady comes to the door, sees the groceries, and starts praising and thanking God. The next door neighbor jumps out and said "Why are you thanking God? I am the one who purchased those groceries for you." The lady said, "Yes, you did, but I asked God for the groceries. I didn't tell him how to get it to me."

Just think about this story. Thoughts? (Jot them down)

God uses unconventional ways to show us who He is. He can use any situation, person, place or thing. As you prepare yourself to Possess your Blessings, remember they may not come conventionally, but they will come just like the walls came down in Jericho. You have walls that are attempting to keep you from possessing everything God has for you, and they, too, will fall, likely unconventionally.

Day 55

Scripture

"The humble will possess the land and will live in peace and prosperity."

- Psalm 37:11

Prayer

Dear God,

Help me to be humble.

Let me possess all that You have promised me before the foundations of the earth.

Let me live in peace and prosperity in all areas of my life.

Reflection: Use space below to jot down your thoughts.

Day 56

Scripture

"Look, I am giving all this land to you! Go in and occupy it, for it is the land the Lord swore to give to your ancestors Abraham, Isaac, and Jacob, and to all their descendants."

- Deuteronomy 1:8

Prayer

Dear God,

I thank You for the land You have given me to occupy. Whether it's a new job, a change in careers, more responsibilities, a new home, God filled relationships, finances, children, ministry, a sound mind, marriage etc. I am ready to receive all that You have for me.

Reflection: Use space below to jot down your thoughts.

Day 57

Scripture

"And God blessed them, and God said unto them, be fruitful, and multiply, and replenish the earth, and subdue it: and have dominion over the fish of the sea and over the fowl of the air and over every living thing that moveth upon the earth."

- Genesis 1:28

Prayer

Lord,

Thank you for blessing me. Let me remember to take what You have given me and be fruitful.

Let me take what You have given me and multiply.

Let me take what You have given me and replenish the earth.

Let me take what You have given me and subdue the earth.

Reflection: Use space below to jot down your thoughts.

Day 58

Scripture

"And I will give unto thee, and to thy seed after thee, the land wherein thou art a stranger, all the land of Canaan, for an everlasting possession: and I will be their God."

- Genesis 17:8

Prayer

Dear God,

Thank You for the blessing that is on me and my children. Thank You for the overflow that blesses my family. Thank You for the promise of everlasting possession. Thank You for being my God.

Reflection: Use space below to jot down your thoughts.

Day 59

Scripture

"Let us hold fast the profession of our faith without wavering"

- Hebrews 10:23

Prayer

Lord,

Let me hold fast to the profession of my faith. Help me to not waver even through my trials and challenges.

Reflection: Use space below to jot down your thoughts.

Day 60

Scripture

"David said to the Philistine, 'You come against me with a sword and spear and javelin, but I come against you in the name of the Lord Almighty.'"

- 1 Samuel 17:45

Prayer

Dear God,

Although challenges and obstacles come to distract me from the blessings you have, I am so thankful that the power of Your name will lead me to victory.

Reflection: Use space below to jot down your thoughts.

Day 61

Scripture

"So here I am today, eighty-five years old. I am still as strong today as the day Moses sent me out. I am just as vigorous to go out to battle now as I was then."

- Joshua 14: 10-11

Prayer

Lord,

I thank You that age does not define me. I thank You that I am strong in you no matter my age.

I thank You that I am constantly renewing my mind and spirit.

Reflection: Use space below to jot down your thoughts.

Day 62

Scripture

"Therefore David inquired of the Lord, saying, 'Shall I go and attack these Philistines?'"

- 1 Samuel 23:2

Prayer

Dear Lord,

I know all things work together for those who love You. Let me remember to be slow to anger.

Let me remember to inquire of You, Lord, what I should do to handle tough situations.

Let me inquire of You, Lord, on choosing my battles.

Let me inquire of You, Lord, before I make any major moves in all areas of my life.

Reflection: Use space below to jot down your thoughts.

Day 63

Scripture

"For where two or three are gathered together in My name, there am I in the midst of them."

- Matthew 18:20

Prayer

Dear God,

I thank You for having friends and family who have a relationship with You. I know when we come together in Your name You are with us.

Reflection: Use space below to jot down your thoughts.

Day 64

Scripture

"Then Asa called to the Lord his God and said, 'Lord, there is no one like You to help the powerless against the mighty.'"

- 2 Chronicles 14:11

Prayer

Lord,

Help me to be powerful for the powerless.

Help me to be bold in Your name.

Let me always remember there is no one like You to help me succeed.

Reflection: Use space below to jot down your thoughts.

Day 65

Scripture

"When you ask, you do not receive, because you ask with wrong motives, that you may spend what you get on your pleasures."

- James 4:3

Prayer

Dear Lord,

Let me be aware of my intentions and motives. Let me focus on what will bring You glory rather than my own pleasures.

Reflection: Use space below to jot down your thoughts.

THANK YOU LORD

POSITION OF POWER

"Now to Him who is able to do exceedingly abundantly above all that we ask or think according to the power that works in us."

- *Ephesians 3:20*

Every day we get to decide who or what will have power over us. Some days we will have it all together, and other days we may get pushed to the edge. The great thing is we get to make a decision about how we exercise the position of power that we have inherited through Christ.

Many moons ago, I used to enjoy watching a sitcom called *The Honeymooners*. Ralph Kramden, played by actor Jackie Gleason, was the lead character who had a funny way of trying to control his anger. He would say "pins and needles, needles and pins, a happy man is a man that grins." And then, he would force a fake smile. I remember trying to emulate this little saying when I was upset, but it never really did anything for me, let alone take away whatever negative feelings I was experiencing. It was not until I started to read my word and literally recite The Lord's Prayer over and over and over again that I felt the negative energy leaving me. Now, don't get me wrong, it has taken me years to get this down pact, and, even then, there are times where I miss the mark. That is normal. After all, we are still human beings. The key is not to get down on ourselves. We must allow God to pick us up and get back in line. Let us remember, whatever we feed will grow. We must constantly remind ourselves not to allow anger, social media, news reports, or other people's behavior to have power over us. As children of God, we are in the Position of Power to do exceedingly and abundantly. And, our Position of Power is rooted in our capacity to love.

Day 66

Scripture

"The Lord will fight for you, and you have only to be silent."

- Exodus 14:14

Prayer

Dear God,

Let me always remember that You will fight for me. Help me to guard my mouth and seek guidance from You when I feel like I am being attacked.

Reflection: Use space below to jot down your thoughts.

Day 67

Scripture

"The Word reduces the capacity to sin and strengthens us against temptation."

- Psalm 119:11

Prayer

Dear God,

When my anger is on high and my temper wants to flare up, please let me remember Your word. Strengthen me against temptation. Let me remember that You are in control. You reign supreme over every situation. Even when circumstances try to taunt me, may I remember, because of Jesus, I am the head and not the tail.

Reflection: Use space below to jot down your thoughts.

Day 68

Scripture

"I can do all things through Christ who strengthens me."

- Philippians 4:13

Prayer

Dear God,

I can do all things through Christ who strengthens me.

I can do all things through Christ who strengthens me.

I can do all thing through Christ who strengthens me.

Thank You, God, for this word.

Reflection: Use space below to jot down your thoughts.

Day 69

Scripture

"But you are a chosen race, a royal priesthood, a holy nation, a people for his own possession, that you may proclaim the excellencies of him who called you out of darkness into His marvelous light."

- 1 Peter 2:9

Prayer

Dear God,

Thank You for loving me. May I draw closer to You and lay at your feet, basking in the goodness and greatness You have prepared for me. Let me soak up Your love and rest in Your presence. Let me go into the world and shine with Your light. Let me be a witness to Your unwavering love. There is absolutely nothing I want to do, no decision I want to make, without You.

Reflection: Use space below to jot down your thoughts.

Day 70

Scripture

"And above all things, love each other deeply, because love covers over a multitude of sins."

- 1 Peter 4:8

Prayer

Dear God,

Help me to love more, have more compassion, and live in alignment with Your word.

Help me to remember that I am here to know and honor Your will for my life.

Help me to remember that my life should point to You.

Reflection: Use space below to jot down your thoughts.

Day 71

Scripture

"A fool is quick tempered, but a wise person stays calm when insulted."

- Proverbs 12:16

Prayer

Dear God,

Let me not be a fool that is quick tempered. Help me to be wise and stay calm when insulted. Let my diligent hand rule and lead me on a path to living a rich life in all areas. Let my hard work make me soar to heights unseen, but consciously in a state of humility.

Reflection: Use space below to jot down your thoughts.

Day 72

Scripture

"We love because He first loved us."

- 1 John 4:19

Prayer

Dear God,

There is nothing that I want more than You. There is nothing that I need more than You. I am grateful for what You have given me. You have blessed me with (insert your blessings), but I know these blessings will never love me more than You. So, hear me when I say, "Thank You, Lord. Thank You from the top of my head to the soles of my feet. Thank You with all of my being.'

Reflection: Use space below to jot down your thoughts.

Day 73

Scripture

"I glorify You on earth, having accomplished the work which You have given me to do."

- John 17:4

Prayer

Dear God,

Remind me that my role is to care for those around me and focus on who You assign to me. Help me not to be judgmental as we are all equal in Your eyes. Help me to see the good in all of Your creations. Let me leave the judging to you. Instead, let me concentrate on living to please You and not man. Help me to be who and what You want me to be. Give me strength, faith, and hope. Most of all, give me guidance each and every day. I let go and give You control.

Reflection: Use space below to jot down your thoughts.

Day 74

Scripture

"The end of something is better than its beginning. Patience is better than pride."

- Ecclesiastes 7:8

Prayer

Father God,

You are the God whose promises are sure. Lord, give me patience. Help me to remain in Your will when I try to move ahead on my own. Lord, thank You for all the times You protected me from what I thought I wanted, but You knew were wrong for me. Bring those times of protection to my remembrance when I become anxious.

Reflection: Use space below to jot down your thoughts.

Day 75

Scripture

"For this very reason do your best to add goodness to your faith; to your goodness add knowledge; to your knowledge add self-control; to your self-control add endurance; to your endurance add godliness; to your godliness add Christian affection; and to your Christian affection add love. These are the qualities you need, and if you have them in abundance, they will make you active and effective in your knowledge of our Lord Jesus Christ."

- 2 Peter 1:5-8

Prayer

Dear God,

Guide me.

Direct me.

Prepare me.

Sustain me.

Cover me.

Build me.

Remind me.

Open the door for me.

Give me wisdom.

Protect me.

Provide for me.

Show me.

Let me.

Make me.

Feed me.

Nourish me.

Care for me.

Hold me.

Mold me.

Push me.

Soothe me.

Talk to me.

Walk with me.

Amuse me.

Let me be a blessing and give You all the glory.

Reflection: Use space below to jot down your thoughts.

THANK YOU LORD

FROM PRUNING TO PRODUCING

"Yes, I am the vine; you are the branches. Those who remain in Me, and I in them, will produce much fruit. For apart from Me you can do nothing."

- *John 15:5*

According to Wikipedia, pruning entails specifically removing diseased, damaged, dead, non-productive, unwanted tissue from crop and landscape plants. This same practice can be applied to our lives as we pray to move forward with producing and living our best lives for God.

Think about some things that need pruning in your life (relationships, career, bad habits, etc.)

As you begin to pray for things that are not of God to be removed from your life, you will begin to feel more at peace, a little lighter, and less stressed. Letting go of people, places, and things that are no longer productive in our lives takes time and may not feel good, but it is necessary for you to grow. I assure you, the end result will be far better than the things you had to release.

What fruit do you want to bear? What do you want to flourish? What kind of relationships do you want to have? How do you want to make a difference in your family, community, your world?

Day 76

Scripture

"That is why I tell you not to worry about everyday life- Whether you have enough food and drink, or enough clothes to wear. Isn't life more than food, and body more than clothing? Look at the birds, they don't plant or harvest or store food in barns, for your heavenly father feeds them. Aren't you far more valuable to Him than they are? Can all your worries add a single moment to your life?"

- Mathew 6:25-27

Prayer

Dear God,

Help me get to a place of not worrying. Just like You take care of the birds and the lilies in the field, I know that You will take care of me. I am Your creation and I am valuable to You.

Reflection: Use space below to jot down your thoughts.

Day 77

Scripture

"So we can say with confidence, 'The Lord is my helper, so I will not fear. What can mere people do to me?'"

- Hebrews 13:6

Prayer

Dear God,

You are my helper, and there is nothing for me to fear.

Reflection: Use space below to jot down your thoughts.

Day 78

Scripture

"We use God's mighty weapons, not worldly weapons, to knock down the strongholds of human reasoning and destroy false arguments. We destroy every proud obstacle that keeps people from knowing God. We capture their rebellious thoughts and teach them to obey Christ."

- 2 Corinthians 10:4-5

Prayer

Dear God,

Let me remember that Your weapons are far greater than the weapons of this world. Anything and everything that is not of You in my life will be knocked down according to Your word. Let me remember to use Your word and teach the obstacles to obey Christ.

Reflection: Use space below to jot down your thoughts.

Day 79

Scripture

"Then Jesus got into the boat and started across the lake with His disciples. Suddenly, a fierce storm struck the lake, with waves breaking into the boat. Bust Jesus was sleeping. The disciples went and woke him up shouting, 'Lord, save us! We're going to drown!' Jesus responded, 'Why are you afraid? You have so little faith!' Then He got up and rebuked the wind and waves, and suddenly there was great calm."

- Matthew 8:23-26

Prayer

Dear God,

When the winds and waves of life get me anxious, let me remember how You used your powerful word to calm them. Let me remember to have faith through every struggle whether in my family life or career.

Reflection: Use space below to jot down your thoughts.

Day 80

Scripture

"So now there is no condemnation for those who belong to Christ Jesus."

- Romans 8:1

Prayer

Dear God,

Let me remember that condemnation comes from the enemy. It promotes hopelessness, darkness, destruction, and fear.

Let me remember that conviction comes from You. It is uplifting, full of light, and hopeful. It brings peace and clarity.

Let me remember the difference between the two and run to Your word when experiencing condemnation and confusion.

Reflection: Use space below to jot down your thoughts.

Day 81

Scripture

"For God is not a God of disorder, but of peace, as in all the meetings of God's holy people."

- 1 Corinthians 14:33

Prayer

Dear God,

I thank You for order and peace in my life.

Reflection: Use space below to jot down your thoughts.

Day 82

Scripture

"I have told you all this so that you may have peace in Me. Here on earth you will have many trials and sorrows. But take heart, because I have overcome the world."

- John 16:33

Prayer

Lord,

I have experienced many trials. Let me find my peace in You.

I have experienced many sorrows. Let me find my peace in You.

Let me remember to take heart because You have overcome the world.

Let me find my peace in You.

Reflection: Use space below to jot down your thoughts.

Day 83

Scripture

"Be still, and know that I am God! I will be honored by every nation. I will be honored throughout the world."

- Psalm 46:10

Prayer

Lord,

Today, let me be still and know that You are God!

Reflection: Use space below to jot down your thoughts.

Day 84

Scripture

"The eternal God is your refuge, and His everlasting arms are under you. He drives out the enemy before you; He cries out, destroy them!"

- Deuteronomy 33:27

Prayer

Dear God,

Thank You for being my refuge.

Thank You for Your everlasting arms being under me.

Thank You for driving out my enemy and fighting my battles.

Reflection: Use space below to jot down your thoughts.

Day 85

Scripture

"You will show me the way of life, granting me the joy of Your presence and the pleasures of living with You forever."

- Psalm 16:11

Prayer

Dear God,

Thank You for showing me the way of life.

Thank You for giving me the joy of Your presence.

Thank You for giving me the pleasure of living with You forever.

Reflection: Use space below to jot down your thoughts.

THANK YOU LORD

PRIZED FOR FAVOR

"And may the Lord our God show us His approval and make our efforts successful. Yes, make our efforts successful."

- *Psalm 90:17*

When you are moving forward boldly in faith, you will be met with opportunities to bless others even through your own personal chaos. Pay attention, you may be entertaining angels. Your very presence and words could save somebody's life.

I remember one day I was in a rush and had to make a quick trip to the mall. I ran into a friend who had lost her child to gun violence. I hadn't seen her in a while, aside from texting here and there. We exchanged the usual pleasantries, and, because I was in a rush, I was catching up rather quickly, until I said, "How are you?" She said she was fine. I said great, but she quickly admitted her dishonesty. She said she was depressed and without direction. Her confession about how she truly felt left me standing there speaking with her for longer than I thought, but there was no way I could speed by her courage to confess her true feelings. We talked and talked and talked until I saw something shift in her eyes. Later that night she text me to say "I am glad I ran into you." And truth be told, I'm glad I ran into her too. God does this, you know. He will set up your path to cross with people He needs you to connect with at just the right time. His favor was in that moment. His favor was with us to bless each other from behind the screen of a phone. His favor made what He needed to happen in that moment successful.

Day 86

Scripture

"For even the Son of Man came not to be served but to serve others and to give His life as a ransom for many."

- Mark 10:45

Prayer

Dear God,

Let me always remember that even the Son of Man came not to be served but to serve others.

Reflection: Use space below to jot down your thoughts.

Day 87

Scripture

"But He was pierced for our rebellion, crushed for our sins. He was beaten so we could be whole. He was whipped so we could be healed."

- Isaiah 53:5

Prayer

Dear God,

I don't think I will ever fully understand all that You had to endure for me.

Thank You for Your love and sacrifice.

Because of You, I truly believe I am worth it!

Because of Your sacrifice, I will honor You through worship.

Use me as a vessel to be a light in a room of darkness.

Reflection: Use space below to jot down your thoughts.

Day 88

Scripture

"The steadfast love of the Lord never ceases; His mercies never come to an end; they are new every morning; great is Your faithfulness."

- Lamentations 3:22-23

Prayer

Dear God,

Thank You for waking me up this morning.

I am so grateful that Your love never stops.

I am so grateful that Your mercies never come to an end.

I am so grateful for Your faithfulness.

Reflection: Use space below to jot down your thoughts.

Day 89

Scripture

"You are the light of the world – like a city on a hilltop that cannot be hidden. No one lights a lamp then puts it under a basket. Instead, a lamp is place on a stand where it gives light to everyone in the house. In the same way, let your good deeds shine out for all to see so that everyone will praise your heavenly Father."

- Mathew 5:14-16

Prayer

Dear God,

Today let Your light shine through me for all to see and may everyone I bless praise You for the good deeds that I do.

Reflection: Use space below to jot down your thoughts.

Day 90

Scripture

"The Lord replied to Moses, 'I will indeed do what you have asked, for I look favorably on you, and I know you by name.'"

- Exodus 33:17

Prayer

Dear God,

I am so glad You look favorably upon me and know me by name.

Reflection: Use space below to jot down your thoughts.

Day 91

Scripture

"He will judge everyone according to what they have done. He will give eternal life to those who keep on doing good, seeking after the glory and honor and immortality that God offers."

- Romans 2:6

Prayer

Dear God,

Today let me remember to focus on the things I need to do and not what others are doing. I know that I will be judged according to my works and not the works of others.

Reflection: Use space below to jot down your thoughts.

Day 92

Scripture

"Don't copy the behavior and customs of this world, but let God transform you into a new person by changing the way you think. Then you will learn to know God's will for you, which is good and pleasing and perfect."

- Roman 12:2

Prayer

Lord,

Today, let me remember not to do as this world does, but to allow You to transform me by changing my way of thinking.

Let my transformation focus on what is good.

Let my transformation focus on what is pleasing.

Let my transformation focus on what is perfect.

Reflection: Use space below to jot down your thoughts.

Day 93

Scripture

"For you were slaughtered, and your blood has ransomed people for God from every tribe and language and people and nation. And you have caused them to become a kingdom of priests for our God. And they will reign on the earth."

- Revelation 5:9-10

Prayer

Dear God,

Words will never be able to express my gratitude for the blood You shed for me.

Because of You I am joint heir to the Kingdom.

And according to Your word, I have the authority to reign here on earth.

Reflection: Use space below to jot down your thoughts.

Day 94

Scripture

"Since God chose you to be the holy people He loves, you must clothe yourselves with tenderhearted mercy, kindness, humility, gentleness, and patience. Make allowance for each other's faults, and forgive anyone who offends you. Remember, the Lord forgave you, so you must forgive others."

- Colossians 3:12-13

Prayer

Lord,

Let me clothe myself with mercy, kindness, gentleness and patience.

Let me practice forgiveness as You have forgiven me.

Reflection: Use space below to jot down your thoughts.

Day 95

Scripture

"All praise to God, the Father of our Lord Jesus Christ. God is our merciful Father and the source of all comfort. He comforts us in all our troubles so that we can comfort others. When they are troubled, we will be able to give them the same comfort God has given us."

- 2 Corinthians 1:3-4

Prayer

Dear God,

Thank You for being the source of my comfort so that I can be a comfort for others in their time of need.

Reflection: Use space below to jot down your thoughts.

Day 96

Scripture

"Yet we hear that some of you are living idle lives, refusing to work and meddling in other people's business. We command such people and urge them in the name of the Lord Jesus Christ to settle down and work to earn their own living."

- 2 Thessalonians 3:10-12

Prayer

Dear God,

Let me not live an idle life.

Let me not refuse to use the talents and gifts that you have given me.

Let me focus on Your will always.

Reflection: Use space below to jot down your thoughts.

Day 97

Scripture

"May God give you more and more grace and peace as you grow in your knowledge of God and Jesus our Lord."

- 2 Peter 1:2

Prayer

Lord,

Today I just want to thank You for Your grace and peace as I continue to grow in my knowledge of You and my Lord and savior Jesus.

Reflection: Use space below to jot down your thoughts.

Day 98

Scripture

"You crown the year with a bountiful harvest; even the hard pathways overflow with abundance.

- Psalm 65:11

Prayer

Dear God,

I am thankful for a bountiful year of harvest and although the pathway will not be easy, Your word says it will still overflow with abundance.

Reflection: Use space below to jot down your thoughts.

Day 99

Scripture

"And I will make an everlasting covenant with them: I will never stop doing good for them. I will put a desire in their hearts to worship Me, and they will never leave Me."

- Jeremiah 32:40

Prayer

Lord,

Thank You for Your everlasting covenant.

Thank You for Your promise to never stop doing good for me.

Thank You for putting the desire in my heart to worship You.

Thank You for this eternal relationship.

Reflection: Use space below to jot down your thoughts.

Day 100

Scripture

"For His anger lasts only a moment, but His favor lasts a lifetime. Weeping may last through the night, but joy comes in the morning."

- Psalm 30:5

Prayer

Dear God,

Your word is honorable.

Your word is truth.

Your word brings hope when I feel hopeless.

Your word gives me life.

Your word never changes.

Your word helps me to grow.

Your word is the ultimate blueprint for living.

Thank You for Your lifetime of favor.

And while I may shed tears at night, I am blessed to know that with You joy will be waiting for me in the morning.

Reflection: Use space below to jot down your thoughts.

THANK YOU LORD

EXTRA PRAYERS

Relationships

Scripture

Walk with the wise and become wise, associate with fools and get in trouble.

- Proverbs 13:20

Prayer

Dear God,

Enlarge my circle of friends to include men and women who are wise. Help me to connect with people who are smarter than I and can help elevate me to where You have predestined me to go.

Interceding for Others

Dear God,

I come humbly before you praying on behalf of ________________________________. Lord, please give ___________________________ clarity, release their mind from any strong holds. Release them from anything that is not of You. Guide them, O God, be their light. Give them a quick turnaround so that those who see _______________________________ know they are a child of the most high God. Lord, help __________________________________ to be great. Put the right people who have a true heart for you in their life. Show ____________________ who you are. Let __________ fall to their knees like Paul did on the road to Damascus. Lord, let ________________________________ know that their help comes from You. There is no greater love than the Love of God. I thank You in advance for never leaving or forsaking __________________. May they grow in love right now. For I know that You, and You alone, can turn and make a blind man see.

Relationships

Scripture

"Then, after Job had prayed for his friends, the Lord made him prosperous again and gave him twice as much as he had."

– Job 42: 10

Prayer

Lord,

I come humbly before You, praying for my friends like Job prayed for his friends.

Bless my friends, Lord, beyond their imagination.

Relationships

Dear God,

I don't take my role as a role model lightly.

I do realize that my family, friends, and others look to me for guidance.

I just pray they see Your light in me in the midst of darkness.

I pray for Your guidance and all of my blessings You have for me,

So that I may be a blessing.

Prayer for Husband

Dear God,

I thank You for my husband ______________________ or Future Husband.

I thank You that he has a heart to provide for his family. I ask that You draw him closer to You. I ask that I am the help mate he needs me to be. Oh God, I ask that You give him the resources he needs. I ask that You give him wisdom and discernment. Lord, surround him with men who have a heart for You and who can encourage him to be a great husband/father. Help him to build positive relationships. Help him to make a positive impact on others. Move him to be the man You birthed him to be.

Interceding for spouse

Dear God,

I pray that ______________________________
lives in accordance with Your plan for his/her life.

That he/she would continue to lead and that You will be glorified in our marriage. Lord, that You will bless his/her work. That he/she would lean on the Lord in his/her trials. I pray for his/her integrity. I pray that he/she will walk away from temptation and have a giving heart. I pray for his/her discernment in handling finances, that he/she would trust Your plans for his/her life, not his/her own. I pray that he/she would give everything to the Lord in prayer, that he/she would seek wisdom. I pray that God will teach him/her how to be a good spouse. I pray he/she will submit his/her fears to You. I pray he/she fully grasps his/her purpose and I pray for his/her health and strength. I pray that he/she will be surrounded by the people who bring him/her up. I pray that he/she would boldly declare the truth of the gospel. I pray that he/she would grow spiritually through reading, studying, and prayer. I pray that he/she would have a humble, teachable spirit. I pray that he/she would be full of patience and peace. I pray that he/she would be quick to forgive and for his/her future.

Prayer for Child/Children

Dear God,

Thank you for the gift you have given me _______________________________(place child/children name on line) natural, foster, adopted etc..

Lord, I ask that my child/children have a heart for You. That he/she obey their mother and father. That he/she excel in school. That he/she is a leader. Lord, help me to see the plans that You have for my child that I may guide them in the right direction. I ask that every move he/she makes from now on is guided by You in the direction of their destiny and dreams. I ask for doors of opportunity to open up, from elementary school, middle school, high school, college, and beyond. When people see _______________________________, let them see you. May he/she be in excellent health. May he/she be a true giver to those less fortunate. May he/she be wise and use discernment. Lord, surround my child/children _______________________________ with people who have a heart for You. May he/she grow to know Your word and have an amazing relationship with You.

Family

Dear God,

Please guide my family. Show them who You are. Surround them with loving people who know You. Give them grace and peace. Anything that is not of you must go!

Write down the names of your family members below.

Prayer for Marriage

Dear God,

I come humbly before You, praying for my marriage and the marriage of my friends and family. God, what You have joined together let no one separate. Lord, above all, let us love each other deeply, because love covers a multitude of sins. God, let us, wives and husbands, be completely humble and gentle. Let us be patient, bearing with one another in love. Let us make every effort to keep the unity of the spirit through the bond of peace. God, let us be kind to one another, tenderhearted, forgiving one another, even as God in Christ forgave us. Lord, let us love one another, for love is from You, and whoever loves has been born of God and knows God. Anyone who does not love does not know God because God is Love. Lord, let us trust in You with all our hearts and lean not on our own understanding. Let us acknowledge You in all of our ways so that You will make our paths straight. Let us be strong and courageous. Let us not be frightened or dismayed, knowing that You are with us wherever we go. For we know that all things work together for those who love You God and those who are called according to Your purpose. Because, God, in Your word You said You know the plans that You have for us, plans to prosper, and not to harm us; Plans to give us hope and a future. Lord, we believe you.

Be The Spark

Let me be the Spark that sparks the light in my family.

Let me be the flicker of hope in dark places.

Let me shine so bright like the sun and the Son.

Let me do the works that You have birthed me to do.

And when my eyes close for eternal rest, You will say,

"Well done."

- By Fatima Scipio

If you ask any woman who has taken the leap of faith to live a purposeful life how they did it, they all would say it starts with taking control over the way you think, speak, and treat other people. Now, you can do the same as they do and reign in the new economy! *Boss Lady* is the perfect read that will teach you how to develop a boss lady mindset using the word of God. Fatima Scipio takes her personal experiences and teaches you how to use your thinking power to bring forth the life you were created to live. In this interactive book, you'll learn how to speak with authority and walk with confidence in your God-given knowledge, skills, and abilities. You'll find practical principles that will activate your creativity along with strategies that can be used daily on your journey to living a prosperous life. The life principles in this book will give you a better insight to yourself and will assist you with taking your life to the next level.

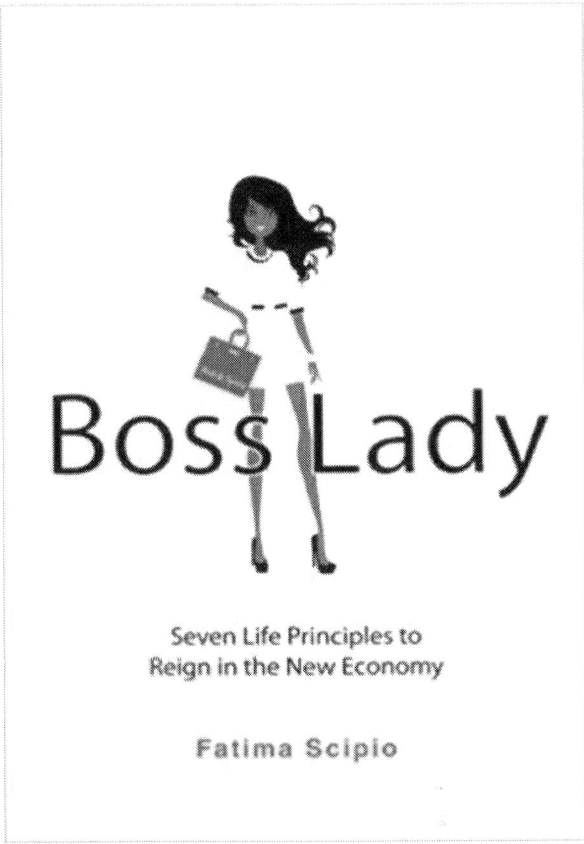

www.fatimascipio.com

Fatima Scipio

Everyone was created with purpose. When people decide to work in that purpose, it becomes their life's work. Life work requires grit and grace. This book provides each individual with tools to harness their skills and work in their purpose.

www.Karensthilaire.com

This book will become your daily companion as you use the reflective and creative practices to discover who you are at the core. This book gives people who have dismissed the idea of being creative a second chance. Most of us were robbed of our creativity when we were told to color inside the lines. *Naked* reminds us that we are made in the image of God, and He is the Master Creator. You will soar as you make a choice to doodle your thoughts, engage in literary and poetic writings, and complete meditative activities. Forty was used several times throughout the Bible as a testing time, and as a result, change occurred.

Naked has forty days of authentic truth telling, and no matter where you are in the process of change, you'll never have to remain stuck when you ART (activate right thinking). *Naked* is a book where biblical principles meet creative practices, inspiring you to push toward your creative core and operate from your self-wealth.

NAKED

STRIPPING TO THE CORE IN 40 DAYS

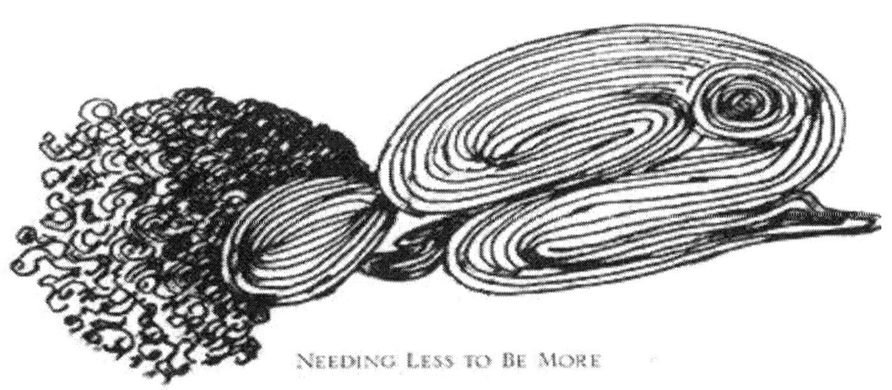

NEEDING LESS TO BE MORE

DENA MCMILLON-BILLUPS

www.Denabillups.com

31702283R00133

Made in the USA
Columbia, SC
02 November 2018